THE
NONNEGOTIABLE
GOSPEL

{ D A V E   H U N T }

BEND · OREGON

THE NONNEGOTIABLE GOSPEL
by Dave Hunt

©1998, 2014 by The Berean Call
5th Edition
ISBN-13: 978-1-928660-43-9

Scripture quotations are from:
The Holy Bible, King James Version

Printed in the United States of America

For information:

THE BEREAN CALL
POST OFFICE BOX 7019
BEND, OREGON 97708-7020

For I am persuaded, that neither death, nor life,
nor angels, nor principalities, nor powers, nor things
present, nor things to come, Nor height, nor depth,
nor any other creature, shall be able to separate us from
the love of God, which is in Christ Jesus our Lord.

—Romans 8:38, 39

◇◇◇◇◇◇◇◇◇◇◇◇◇◇◇◇◇◇◇◇◇◇◇

Contents

Go ye into all the world, and preach the gospel . . . for it is the power of God unto salvation to every one that believeth [it].

—MARK 16:15, ROMANS 1:16

◇◇◇◇◇◇◇◇◇◇◇◇◇◇◇◇◇◇◇◇◇

THE GOSPEL *of* GOD

What is the "good news" of *the* gospel—and from what does it save us?

In order to answer that question, we must begin in the Garden, for it was there, in the most perfect environment that God's heart of love and His creative power could design, that sin had its awful beginning.

Surrounded by beauty, satisfied by abundance, and enjoying the fellowship of their Creator Friend, our first parents nevertheless fell to the seductive lies of the Serpent. "Ye shall be as gods" was Satan's promise, while Adam, in loyalty to Eve, whom he loved more than God himself, joined in her disobedience and ate of the forbidden fruit (1 Timothy 2:14). Thus, "by [this] one man sin entered into the world, and death by sin; and so death passed upon all men, for that all have sinned" (Romans 5:12).

Death not only ends this short earthly life; it separates the sinner from God forever. In His infinite foreknowledge, wisdom, and love, however, God had already planned how He would restore life and reunite mankind with Himself. Without ceasing to be God, He would become a man through a virgin birth. Only God could be the Savior (Isaiah 43:11; 45:21, etc.), thus the Messiah had to be God (Isaiah 9:6; Isaiah 45:15; Titus 1:3, 4, etc.). He would die for our sins to pay the penalty demanded by His justice: " 'Tis mystery all, the *immortal* dies!" hymn writer Charles Wesley declared. Then He would rise from the dead to live in those who would believe in and receive Him as their Lord and Savior. Forgiveness of sins and eternal life would be theirs as a *free gift of His grace*.

Centuries before His incarnation, God inspired the Old Testament prophets to declare His eternal and unchangeable plan of salvation. Definitive criteria were provided by which the coming Savior would be identified. Jesus and His apostles did not invent a "new religion." Christianity fulfills scores of specific prophecies and is therefore provable from Scripture!

So it was not a new gospel that Paul the apostle preached, but "the gospel of God (which he had promised afore by his prophets in the holy scriptures,) concerning his Son Jesus Christ . . ." (Romans 1:1-3). Thus the Bereans could check Paul's message against the Old Testament (Acts 17:11); and he could use the Hebrew prophets, which were read in the synagogue each sabbath, to show that Jesus was the promised Messiah (verses 2, 3). Not Buddha, not Muhammad, not anyone else—only Christ has the required credentials! The fulfillment of scores of specific prophecies in the life, death, and resurrection of Jesus of Nazareth should be absolute proof that He is the true and only Savior.

In Hebrews 2:3, the vital question is asked, "How shall we escape, if we neglect so great salvation?" The answer is so starkly plain; there is no escape. The Bible makes that solemn fact abundantly clear. To reject, add to, take from, or otherwise pervert or embrace a *substitute* for "the gospel of God" is to perpetuate the rebellion begun by Adam and Eve and to leave one eternally separated from God and His proffered salvation.

No wonder Paul wrote, "Knowing therefore the terror of the Lord, we persuade men . . . " (2 Corinthians 5:11). So must we, too, persuade men through the gospel!

The "gospel of your salvation" (Ephesians 1:13) "wherein ye stand; by which also ye are saved" (1 Corinthians 15:1, 2) is simple and precise, leaving no room for misunderstanding or negotiation: "that Christ died for our sins according to the scriptures; and that he was buried, and that he rose again the third day . . . " (verses 3, 4).

This "everlasting gospel" (Revelation 14:6) was promised "before the world began" (2 Timothy 1:9; Titus 1:2) and cannot change with time or culture. There is no other hope for mankind, no other way to be forgiven and brought back to God except through this "strait gate and narrow way" (Matthew 7:13, 14). Any broader road leads to destruction.

{ *The Gospel's Three Elements* }

The one true "gospel of God's grace," which God offers as our *only* salvation, has three basic elements: 1) who Christ is—fully God and perfect, sinless man in one Person (were He less, He could not be our Savior); 2) who we are—hopeless sinners already condemned to eternal death (or we wouldn't need to be saved); and 3) what Christ's death accomplished—the payment of the full penalty for our sins (any attempt by us to pay *in any way* rejects the Cross).

Christ has commanded us to "preach the gospel [good news!] to every creature [person]" (Mark 16:15). What response is required? Both the desperate question and uncomplicated answer are given to us: "What must I do to be saved? . . . *Believe* on the Lord Jesus Christ, and thou shalt be saved" (Acts 16:30, 31). Neither religion, ritual, nor good works will avail. God calls us to simply *believe*. "For by grace are ye saved through *faith*" (Ephesians 2:8)—whosoever *believes* in him will not perish, but has eternal life (John 3:16).

It is the *gospel* alone that saves those who *believe* it. Nothing else will save. Therefore we must preach the gospel. Paul said, "Woe is unto me, if I preach not the gospel" (1 Corinthians 9:16). Sentimental appeals to "come to Jesus" or "make a decision for Christ" avail nothing if the gospel is not clearly explained and believed.

Many are attracted to Christ because of His admirable character, noble martyrdom, or because He changes lives. Such converts have not believed the *gospel* and thus are not saved. This is the solemn teaching of Scripture (John 3:36)!

Paul said that "the gospel of Christ . . . is the power of God *unto salvation* to every one that believeth" (Romans 1:16). He also called it "the gospel . . . by which also *ye are saved*" (1 Corinthians 15:1, 2); and "the gospel of *your salvation*" (Ephesians 1:13). Clearly, from these and other scriptures, salvation comes *only* through *believing the gospel*. Christ told His disciples to go into "all the world, and preach the gospel" (Mark 16:15), a gospel which the Bible precisely defines.

Salvation comes on God's terms and by His grace, and we negotiate the gospel neither with God nor with one another. "The Father sent the Son to be the Saviour of the world" (1 John 4:14). Salvation is a work of God and His Son. We either believe it or reject it. We don't "dialogue" about it.

It is also called the "gospel of Christ" (Mark 1:1; Romans 1:16; 15:19; 1 Corinthians 9:12, 18; 2 Corinthians 4:4; 9:13; 10:14; Galatians 1:7; Philippians 1:27; 1 Thessalonians 3:2; 2 Thessalonians 1:8). He is the Savior, and salvation is His work, not ours, as the angels said: "For unto you is born this day in the city of David a Saviour, which is Christ the Lord" (Luke 2:11).

Paul specifies the gospel that saves: "that Christ died for our sins according to the scriptures; and that he was buried, and that he rose again the third day according to the scriptures" (1 Corinthians 15:3, 4). "I am the door," said Christ: "by *me* if any man enter in, he shall be saved" (John 10:9).

The gospel contains nothing about baptism, church membership or attendance, tithing, sacraments or rituals, diet, or clothing. If we add *anything* to the gospel, we have perverted it and thus come under Paul's anathema in Galatians 1:8, 9!

The gospel is all about what Christ has done. It says nothing about what Christ must yet do because the work of our redemption is finished. "Christ *died* for our sins." His was a past act, never to be repeated, for Christ triumphantly declared, "It is *finished*" (John 19:30)!

Nor does it say anything about what *we* must do, because we can do nothing. "Not by works of righteousness which we have done, but according to his mercy he saved us" (Titus 3:5); "for by grace are ye saved through faith . . . the gift of God (is) not of works, lest any man should boast . . . " (Ephesians 2:8, 9).

Instead of works, the gospel requires faith. It is the power of God unto salvation to those who *believe*. "But to him that *worketh not*, but *believeth* on him that justifieth the ungodly, his *faith* is counted for righteousness" (Romans 4:5) . . . "that whosoever believeth in him should not perish, but have everlasting life" (John 3:16).

The gospel is a two-edged sword. It declares, "He that believeth on the Son hath everlasting life." The same verse also says, "and he that believeth not the Son shall not see life; but the wrath of God abideth on him" (John 3:36).

{ *The Difficult Part* }

Right here we come to the most difficult part of the gospel to accept—that those who do not believe it are eternally lost, no matter what good works they do.

The reasons for that fact are grounded in both God's love and His justice. God's justice requires that the infinite penalty for sin must be paid. In payment we would be separated from God forever, so He became a man through the virgin birth to pay the penalty for us. No one can complain against God. He has proved His love by doing all He could for our salvation. He has himself paid the penalty and on that basis can be both "just, and the justifier of him which believeth in Jesus" (Romans 3:26).

Christ pleaded in the Garden, "if it be possible (i.e., if there is any other way mankind can be saved), let this cup pass from me" (Matthew 26:39). We know that there is no other way or God would not have required His beloved Son to bear the full brunt of His wrath against sin. The fact that men nailed Christ to the cross would only condemn us. But on the cross, when man was doing his worst to his Creator, Christ paid the penalty for our sins in full.

Only if we accept that payment on our behalf can we be saved. "[T]here is none other name under heaven given among men, whereby we *must* be saved" (Acts 4:12); "what *must* I do to be saved?

. . . Believe on the Lord Jesus Christ, and thou shalt be saved" (Acts 16:30, 31).

To "believe on the Lord Jesus Christ" includes *who* He *is* and *what* He *has done*.

Jesus said, ". . . Ye are from beneath; I am from above . . . if ye believe not that I AM [this is God's name, Yahweh], ye shall die in your sins" (John 8:23, 24). Jesus himself says we must believe that He is God, for He is; and no one less than God could save us. We must believe that the sinless One "died for our sins," and was buried; and that He rose bodily from the grave. Only by believing this gospel are we saved. So says God's Word.

Why could not even a Mother Teresa get to heaven by good works? Because we are all sinners; and because once we have broken one of God's commandments we "[are] guilty of all" (James 2:10); and "by the deeds of the law there shall no flesh be justified in his sight" (Romans 3:20). Keeping the law perfectly from now on could never make up for having already broken it.

For God to grant salvation by any other means than faith in Christ alone would be an insult to the One whom the Father insisted had to endure His wrath as the sacrifice for sin. Furthermore, God would be breaking His own code of justice and going back on His Word. No, even God himself could not save earth's most notable "saint." Christ's blood avails only for repentant sinners.

Oswald Chambers warned lest, in our zeal to get people to accept the gospel, we manufacture a gospel acceptable to people and produce "converts" who are not saved. Today's most popular perversion is the "positive" gospel, which is designed to offend no one with truth. One of our most popular televangelists, for example, has said that it is demeaning to call anyone a sinner and that Christ died to restore human dignity and self-esteem. He claims to win many to Christ with that seductive message—but such a gospel does not *save sinners.*

Evangelistic appeals are often made to "come to Christ" for the wrong reasons: in order to be healthy, happy, successful, to restore a marriage, or to handle stress. Others preach a gospel that is so diluted or perverted that it deceives many into thinking they are saved. No fraud could be worse, for the consequences are eternal!

Religion, not atheism, is Satan's main weapon. "The god of this world hath blinded the minds of them which believe not, lest the light of the glorious gospel of Christ . . . should shine unto them" (2 Corinthians 4:4). To combat "the gospel of the grace of God" (Acts 20:24), the great deceiver has many false gospels, but they all have two subtle rejections of grace in common: ritual and/or self-effort.

Ritual makes redemption an ongoing process performed by a special priesthood; and self-effort gives man a part to play in earning his salvation. The one denies the finality of the Cross. The other denies its sufficiency. Either one robs God of the uniqueness of the gift He wishes to bestow upon fallen man: "For the wages of sin is death; but the gift of God is eternal life through Jesus Christ our Lord" (Romans 6:23). †

THUS, AMAZINGLY, MAN'S REBELLION AGAINST GOD IS SEEN MOST CLEARLY IN HIS RELIGIONS, ALL OF WHICH ARE BUT MIRROR IMAGES OF BABEL—INGENIOUS AND PERSISTENT ATTEMPTS TO 'CLIMB UP SOME OTHER WAY' INSTEAD OF ENTERING THROUGH THE DOOR THAT GOD HAS PROVIDED IN HIS SON.

An altar of earth thou shalt make unto me. . . . And if thou wilt make me an altar of stone, thou shalt not build it of hewn stone: for if thou lift up thy tool upon it, thou hast polluted it. Neither shalt thou go up by steps unto mine altar, that thy nakedness be not discovered thereon.

—Exodus 20:24-26

. . . [L]et us build us a city and a tower [of Babel], whose top may reach unto heaven . . .

Genesis 11:4

MERCY vs. WORKS

No two tenets of faith could be more opposed to one another than those presented above.

On the one hand, we have God's rejection of any human effort to buy salvation or His favor. If man is to come to God, it must be solely by His grace and His provision, not by any human work.

On the other hand, we see man's flagrant repudiation of God's prohibition against self-effort, and his arrogant attempt to build a tower that would enable him to climb by steps of his own making into heaven itself.

God's instructions were explicit. If the ground was too rocky to gather up a mound of earth for an altar, stones could be heaped together—but they could not be cut, fashioned, or polished with a tool. Nor could the altar be elevated. Not one step must be climbed to reach it. There must be no illusion that man could contribute anything by his own efforts to his salvation. God himself is the only One who can save man, and salvation must be a gift of His grace. Such is the gospel consistently presented from Genesis to Revelation. Consider the following:

> I, even I, am the Lord; and beside me there is *no saviour* (Isaiah 43:11); For unto us a child [the Messiah] is born . . . [He is] The mighty God, The everlasting Father (Isaiah 9:6). . . . thou shalt call his name Jesus: for *he shall save his people from their sins* (Matthew 1:21). . . . *they that are in the flesh cannot please God* (Romans 8:8). For by grace are ye saved . . . *not of works*, lest any man should boast (Ephesians 2:8, 9); *Not by works* of righteousness which we have done, but according to his *mercy* he saved us (Titus 3:5); Being justified freely *by his grace* through

the redemption that is in Christ Jesus (Romans 3:24); And if by grace, then is it no more of works: otherwise grace is no more grace. But if it be of works, then is it no more grace: otherwise work is no more work. (Romans 11:6)

It was the incredible act of rebellion in Eden against the Almighty that separated man from his Creator. No less astonishing is the fact that man continues his defiance in his very attempts to be reconciled to God—and so persists in his self-righteous resolve to contribute *something* toward his salvation.

Thus, amazingly, man's rebellion against God is seen most clearly in his religions, all of which are but mirror images of Babel—ingenious and persistent attempts to "climb up some other way" instead of entering through the door that God has provided in His Son (John 10:1).

Babel may be traced from ancient paganism to the "high places" (elevated altars) of heathen worship adopted by Israel (Leviticus 26:30; 1 Kings 11:7; 2 Kings 23:15; Ezekiel 16:24-39, etc.) and on to every religion on earth today. The ornate temples or mosques and elaborate ceremonies found in Islam, Hinduism, Buddhism, Mormonism, and other cults and the occult are obvious continuations of Babel. So are the magnificent cathedrals, lofty steeples, exalted and gilded altars, luxurious vestments, and impressive rituals of today's "high church" denominations.

Such pomp turns off many non-Christians who rightly want nothing to do with a God who is influenced by fleshly enhancements.

But was not Solomon's temple most magnificent? Yes, but it was uniquely designed and commanded by God. Both the tabernacle in the wilderness and the temple which succeeded it were "a figure [picture] . . . of good things to come [i.e., of Christ and heaven]" (Hebrews 9:9-11). God said to Moses, "See . . . that thou make all things according to the pattern shewed to thee in the mount [Sinai]" (Hebrews 8:5).

No such pattern or approval was given by God for any other religious structure. Although Protestants reject relics, statues and icons, they often refer to their places of worship as "sanctuaries," as though God dwells there. In fact, God inhabits the Christian's body ("your body is the temple of the Holy Ghost" —1 Corinthians 3:17; 6:19), which is therefore to be kept holy. Paul reminded the Athenians:

> God that made the world and all things therein,
> seeing that he is Lord of heaven and earth, dwel-
> leth not in temples made with hands; Neither
> is worshipped with men's hands, as though he
> needed any thing, seeing he giveth to all life,
> and breath, and all things. . . . (Acts 17:24, 25)

Jesus explained that God does, indeed, desire our worship—but it must be "in spirit and in truth" (John 4:23, 24). Affectations, whether in physical adornments, props or ceremonies, appeal to the flesh and, far from enhancing worship, deny both the truth and the Spirit, by which it alone can be offered to the God who created and redeemed us. Sacramentalism—the belief that liturgy's form and formulas transmit spiritual power and that salvation comes through the sacraments—too readily creeps into even Protestant thinking. In fact, some still believe that baptism saves and that taking the bread and cup brings life, etc.

Alas, we are all Eve's children by nature and still prone to follow the ways of Cain and Babel. Every place of worship that has been adorned for the purpose of hallowing it or gaining God's favor or making worship more acceptable violates Exodus 20:24-26 as well as the rest of Scripture.

All such "sanctuaries" are monuments to man's rebellion and his proud and perverted religion of self-effort.

Unfortunately, it is all too easy to fall into the error of imagining that belonging to a church and periodically "worshiping" in its "sanctuary" makes one a Christian and compensates for one's lack of consistent, personal holiness.

Of course, no one in this day and age is under the illusion that one can climb a physical tower to heaven. Yet the folly of today's religions is every bit as monumental, and the anarchy against God that motivates those beliefs is just as evil as was the Tower of Babel. Billions continue, in the spirit of Babel, to pursue equally futile, self-oriented religious programs, hoping to earn their way to heaven. In the process, *truth* and *doctrine* are relegated to a secondary role, or none.

{ *Faith is Not a "Power"* }

Sadly, for many, faith is a power of the *mind*, and God is merely a placebo that helps one "believe" and thereby activate this mind power. "Prayer is communicating with the deep unconscious. . . . Your unconscious mind . . . [has a] power that turns wishes into realities," says a popular writer. He says further, "You don't know the power you have within you! . . . You make the world into anything you choose." It is Babel again in a more sophisticated form. The power of "thinking" becomes the magic stairway that leads to the paradise where all one's wishes can be fulfilled.

For others, faith is a mind power that even God uses—a force contained in words and released when one speaks forth "the word of faith." "By the spoken word," declares one of their leaders, "we create our universe . . . you create the presence of Jesus with your mouth . . . through visualization and dreaming you can incubate your future and hatch the results." Here we have an evangelical form of Christian Science or Science of Mind!

Many Christians have unwittingly believed a similar lie. They imagine that faith is believing that what they are praying for will happen. Of course, if *believing* something will happen *causes* it to happen, then who needs God? Men themselves have become gods. The power of belief becomes one's tower of Babel, the magic steps by which one climbs to that "state of mind called heaven."

Biblical faith, however, is believing that *God*

will answer one's prayer. That changes everything! I could never truly believe a prayer would be answered—nor would I want it to be—unless I were certain it was God's will. Faith is not a magic power we aim at God to get Him to bless our plans, but "the *obedience* of faith" (Acts 6:7; Romans 1:5; 16:26; 2 Thessalonians 1:8, etc.) brings us into submission to Him as the instruments of His will.

Humanists also have their Babel-like, do-it-yourself religion. They call it science. It, too, reflects man's continued rebellion. Modern man hopes to conquer the atom, space, and all disease and thus to become immortal master of the universe. The materialist's "heaven" is a peaceful cosmos populated by highly evolved, space-traveling civilizations that have restored paradise through supertechnology.

Such was the dream ("to join a community of galactic civilizations . . . [is] our hope in a vast and awesome universe") that President Carter, a professing Christian, expressed to anticipated extraterrestrial contactees on the gold record carried into space by *Voyager* in 1977.

Rank materialism leaves the soul empty, but

adding a touch of religion to science seems to fill the void while keeping faith "rational." There is no more deadly delusion than a scientific religion. It is the delusion of Babel all over again, with advancing knowledge building the steps that both lead man to "heaven" and open to him the very powers of God.

One of Christian psychology's major appeals to evangelicals is its false claim to being scientific. It fails, however, the litmus test of Exodus 20:24-26. Its altars are built of the cut and polished stones of human wisdom; its rituals are not found in Scripture; and self rather than God is the object of worship. Moreover, on its altars burns the strange fire (Leviticus 10:1; Nahum 3:4) of humanistic theories unacceptable to God.

Religious science is a major element in the environmental movement, where the earth is increasingly viewed as sacred. Ecotheology, says a Georgetown University professor, "starts with the premise that the Universe is God." Carl Sagan exemplified today's scientific paganism. "If we must worship a power greater than ourselves," intoned this high priest of cosmos worship, "does it not make sense to revere the Sun and stars?" Here we go again! To draw closer to, and thus better observe and worship, the heavenly bodies was a major purpose of the Tower of Babel.

The environmental movement is a humanistic attempt to restore the lost paradise of Eden without repenting of rebellion against the Creator. Such is the message that is being seductively presented to America's children in the public schools.

New Age is being purposefully promoted in the public schools through such programs as *America 2000*. As governor of Arkansas, Bill Clinton initiated a school reform that had much to do with remolding the students into planetary citizens alienated from parents, including the worship of self and the universe as God.

Exodus 20:24-26 is a foundational passage that makes it clear that the earth is neither to be honored nor worshiped but to be used as an altar. Sin brought a curse upon the earth, a curse that could only be removed through the shedding of blood (Leviticus 17:11). Animals were sacrificed upon an altar of earth in anticipation of the Lamb of God, who would, "by the sacrifice of himself" (Hebrews 9:26), once and for all obtain "eternal redemption for us" (verse 12).

It is for man's own good that God visits sin with death. How horrible it would be for mankind to continue forever in its state of rebellion, thus perpetuating ever-increasing evil, sickness, suffering, sorrow, and death. Only out of death in payment of the full penalty for sin comes resurrection (not reincarnation's amoral recycling of evil) and a whole new universe into which sin and suffering can never enter. Such is God's desire and provision for all mankind. Those who reject the free gift of eternal life offered by His grace will experience eternal regret.

There are peripheral issues on which Christians may differ, such as diet, dress, mode of baptism, honoring certain days, how and how often to keep the Lord's supper, etc. Salvation, however, is the central issue on which all must agree. Paul cursed those who taught that one must believe the gospel *and keep the law* in order to be saved (Galatians 1:6-12). Such a slight addition destroyed the gospel. No one believing that message could be saved! Nor is anyone a Christian who believes one of today's popular diluted gospels.

The "gospel of God," as we have seen, is very specific and must be believed for one to be saved.

"[S]trait is the gate, and narrow is the way, which leadeth unto life, and few there be that find it" (Matthew 7:14). That "narrow-minded" statement was not the invention of some dogmatic fundamentalist but came from our Lord himself.

"The faith" for which we must "earnestly contend" (Jude 3) has definite moral and doctrinal content and must be believed for salvation. All else is Babel. ✝

As Jim Elliot, one of the martyrs killed in Ecuador, said when as a young man he chose the mission field over more popular careers, "He is no fool who gives up what he cannot keep to gain what he cannot lose." That choice is only logical if one believes that time is short and eternity endless . . .

Go ye therefore, and [make disciples of]
all nations, . . . Teaching them to observe all things
whatsoever I have commanded you: and, lo,
I am with you alway, even unto the end of the world.

—Matthew 28:19, 20

◇◇◇◇◇◇◇◇◇◇◇◇◇◇◇◇◇◇

The Call *to*
Discipleship

Christ directed His disciples to preach the good news of the gospel to everyone everywhere. This command to His original followers has become known as the "Great Commission." It is stated in two ways: "go ye into all the world, and *preach the gospel*" (Mark 16:15); and *make disciples* (Matthew 28:19, 20). Those who preach the gospel are to disciple those who believe it. Born again by God's Spirit into His family (John 3:3-5; 1 John 3:2), converts begin a new life as Christ's followers, eager to learn of Him and to obey the One to whom they now owe such an infinite debt of gratitude.

Christ warned that some would seem to receive

the gospel with great enthusiasm only to become entangled in the world, discouraged, and disillusioned. They would eventually turn back from following Him. Many maintain a facade of Christianity without inward reality, deceiving perhaps even themselves. Never fully convinced in their hearts, they are unwilling nevertheless to admit their unbelief. "Examine yourselves," Paul warned, "whether ye be in the faith" (2 Corinthians 13:5).

Of those who are genuine, all too few are able to give a *reason* for the hope that is in them (1 Peter 3:15). How many Christians are able to convincingly persuade an atheist, Buddhist, Hindu, or New Ager with overwhelming evidence and sound reason from Scripture? God's Word is the sword of the Spirit, but few know it well enough to quell their own doubts, much less to convert others.

One of today's greatest needs is for the solid Bible teaching that produces disciples who are able to "earnestly contend for the faith once [for all] delivered to the saints" (Jude 3). That faith for which we must contend was delivered by Christ to the original twelve disciples, who were then to teach those whom they evangelized "*to observe all things*" that Christ had commanded them.

Through succeeding generations of those who have been won to Him and who have in turn, in obedience to their Lord, discipled others, this unbroken chain of command comes down to us in our time. Not some special priest or clergy class but each Christian today, like those who have passed before, is a successor to the apostles. Think of what that means!

At the heart of Christ's call to discipleship is the daily application of His cross in each life. Yet one seldom hears in evangelical circles Christ's definitive declaration: "And whosoever doth not bear his cross, and come after me . . . [and] forsaketh not all that he hath, he cannot be my disciple" (Luke 14:27-33). The call to discipleship must be honestly faced. Through the Cross we die to self and begin to live to our Lord in resurrection power (Galatians 2:20). Indeed, Christ's death on the cross would have been a hollow act if it did not bring forth new life, for now and for eternity.

Resurrection life reckons the old life dead and makes no provision for the flesh (Romans 6:4, 11; 13:14). Instead of the popular self-esteem, God calls us to deny self, to love truth and hate folly, to please God instead of others or ourselves, no

matter what the cost in this life. Never mind social
pressures from what others think, say, or do. We
must be fully persuaded that what God thinks and
what He will say when we appear before Him one
day is all that matters.

As Jim Elliot, one of the martyrs killed in
Ecuador, said when as a young man he chose the
mission field over more popular careers, "He is
no fool who gives up what he cannot keep to gain
what he cannot lose." That choice is only logical
if one believes that time is short and eternity
endless. Such commitment brings heavenly joy,
peace, and a fulfillment that nothing earth offers
can rival.

To those whom He called into a saving rela-
tionship with Himself, Christ said, "Follow me"
(Matthew 4:19; 8:22; 9:9; 16:24, etc.). This
simple command, which our Lord repeated after
His resurrection (John 21:19, 22), is as applicable
to Christians today as it was when He called the
first disciples.

{ *Following Christ* }

What does it mean to follow Christ? Did He promise His followers that they would be successful, wealthy, and esteemed in this world?

God may grant earthly success to a few for His own purposes. On the whole, however, our Lord declared that those who were true to Him would follow in His path of rejection and suffering: "If the world hate you, ye know that it hated me before it hated you. . . . The servant is not greater than his lord. If they have persecuted me, they will also persecute you. . . . for my name's sake . . . " (John 15:18-21).

Such was the lot of the early church. Yet today, as the key to "the good life," Christianity is popularized. The idea of suffering for Christ doesn't suit a worldly church. How strange such verses as the following seem to Christians in America: "For unto you it is given in the behalf of Christ, not only to believe on him, but also to suffer for his sake" (Philippians 1:29). Suffering is *given* to us? Paul speaks as though it were a *precious privilege* to suffer for His sake! After being imprisoned and beaten, the early disciples rejoiced "that they were counted worthy to suffer shame for his name" (Acts 5:41). Such is the commitment to which the gospel actually calls us.

Christ told His disciples after the Resurrection, "As my Father hath sent me, even so send I you" (John 20:21). The Father sent the Son as a lamb to the slaughter into a world that would hate and crucify Him! And as the Father sent Him, so Christ sends us into a world that He promises will treat His followers as it did Him. Are we willing? Is this not your idea of Christianity? Then think again, and check it out against the Scriptures. We are further from Him and His truth than we realize!

Peter, who failed so miserably and was restored by the Lord, explained that Christians would be hated, falsely accused, and persecuted, and would be expected to suffer these wrongs patiently (1 Peter 2:19, 20; 4:12-19; etc.). Under the inspiration of the Holy Spirit, he wrote,

> For even hereunto were ye called: because Christ also suffered for us, leaving us an example, that ye should follow his steps: who did no sin, neither was guile found in his mouth: who, when he was reviled, reviled not again; when he suffered, he threatened not; but committed himself to him that judgeth righteously: who his

own self bare our sins in his own body on the tree, that we, being dead to sins, should live unto righteousness. . . . (1 Peter 2:21-25)

Christians are being imprisoned and martyred again in communist China, in Muslim countries, and at the hands of Catholics in Mexico. Similar persecutions could well overtake us in America. Already pastors are being fined and imprisoned and churches locked and sold by the state. In 1986, for example, Jefferson County, Kentucky imposed a licensing fee upon every "business, profession, trade, or occupation"—including pastors and churches.

Recently I listened, with tears welling in my eyes, as my wife, Ruth, read to me some of the stories from her Anabaptist heritage. For being rebaptized after they became Christians (and thus denying the efficacy of Rome's infant baptism), these Anabaptists were burned at the stake. To escape the flames many fled the Inquisition in Holland to Prussia. From there they fled to Russia, and in the closing days of World War II, many attempted an escape from godless and oppressive communism back to the West.

Out of one group of 611 leaving Russia, only 31 arrived back in Holland. Tramping day and night through the snow, unable to find food or shelter, some were caught and returned. Others were killed or died of exposure. Children were torn from parents, husbands from wives. The terror and agony were beyond imagination.

As Ruth read of the indescribable suffering, I thought of the thousands of Christians in America who find it necessary to enter "therapy" and spend months, if not years, dealing with comparatively trifling "hurts from the past." I thought of the thousands of Christian psychologists who encourage their clients to pity themselves, to pamper their "inner child," when what they need is to deny self, take up the cross, and follow Christ!

In contrast, I was inspired by the testimony of those who suffered the loss of possessions, of loved ones, of almost every earthly hope and joy, yet triumphed through their faith in Christ. Going to a "therapist" and engaging in self-pity would have seemed incomprehensible to them when they had the Lord and His Word and when they knew that "our light affliction, which is but for a moment, worketh for us a far more exceeding and eternal weight of glory" (2 Corinthians 4:17)!

{ *The Strength to Stand* }

Whence comes the strength to stand against overwhelming suffering and to triumph as Christ's faithful disciples? Oddly enough, victory comes not through our strength but through our weakness.

When Paul cried out for deliverance from a severe trial, Christ replied that He had allowed it to make Paul weak enough so that he would trust only in the Lord, rather than in his great abilities. "[M]y strength is made perfect in [your] weakness," our Lord promised (2 Corinthians 12:9).

Paul exhorts us, "As ye have therefore received Christ Jesus the Lord, so walk ye in him" (Colossians 2:6). Did we not receive Christ in weakness as helpless, hopeless sinners crying out to Him for mercy and grace? That, then, is the way we are to walk this path of triumph in suffering—as sinners saved by grace, weak and helpless in ourselves, and trusting totally in Him.

We are earthen vessels, but we contain a great treasure: "that the excellency of the power may be of God, and not of us" (2 Corinthians 4:7) Such is the secret of our triumph over the world, the flesh, and the devil. The load is too heavy for us to carry. What a relief to turn it over to Him! And what a joy to be delivered from the fear of man, from seeking to win the acclaim of this world, from seeking anything but His "Well done, thou good and faithful servant" (Matthew 25:21) in that coming day.

Some manage to amass a fortune to leave at death to their heirs. Others have little of this earth's goods but have great riches laid up in heaven for eternity. It takes little wisdom to know who of these have made the wisest choice and who have been truly successful.

God has an eternal purpose for our lives. Our passion should be to know and to fulfill that purpose, beginning here on this earth. One day, very soon, we will each stand before Him. What a tragedy to miss the very purpose for which we were created and redeemed!

You may say, "Yes, I want to be used of God, but I don't know what He wants me to do." Or, "I try to serve Him, try to witness for Him, and it all seems to come to nothing."

Learn this: Greater than anything God can do *through* you is what He wants to do *in* you.

What counts most is not *quantity* but *quality*, not so much your outward effort but your motive within—the purity of your heart rather than your prominence with men.

Moreover, what seems much in time may be very little in eternity. It is not one's talents or energy but the empowering of the Holy Spirit that produces genuine and lasting results: "Not by might, nor by power, but by my spirit, saith the LORD of hosts" (Zechariah 4:6). Trust God for the filling and empowering of His Spirit.

Millions have laid down their lives for the faith. Their commitment to Christ meant so much that they would not compromise when threatened with the most excruciating torture and death. Can we fathom their choice?

The martyrs could have chosen the ecumenical path of compromise, of avoiding controversy and affirming the "common beliefs of all religions," and thus have escaped the flame or the sword. They chose instead to stand firm for the truth, to contend earnestly for the faith.

Christ calls us to do the same.

Paul said he had been "put in trust with the gospel" (1 Thessalonians 2:4). So have each of us. Let us be certain that we keep that trust for the sake of the lost and in honor of our Lord who paid such a price for man's redemption!

There is no escaping the eternal choice that confronts us. Will we follow from afar, or will we seek to follow in our Lord's very footsteps? One day we will give an account before God for the path we choose. What joy there is now and will be eternally in being true to Him! ✝

IN DEFENSE OF THE FAITH: BIBLICAL ANSWERS TO CHALLENGING QUESTIONS —*Dave Hunt*

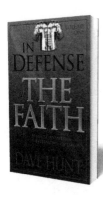

With the keen eye of an experienced treasure hunter, the author helps readers probe and unearth the incredible wealth of guidance found in God's Word. The resulting adventure will not only strengthen the faith of believers but equip them to live daily according to His revealed truth in an increasingly hostile world. Find biblical responses to such questions as:

- Why does God allow suffering and evil?
- What about all the "contradictions" in the Bible?
- Are some people predestined to go to hell?
- Is the Bible reliable?
- Is the Bible the only book of God?

This book tackles the tough issues, including why a merciful God would punish people who have never heard of Christ, and how to tell the difference between God's workings and Satan's. The Berean Call, 347 pages.

ISBN: 1-928660-66-8 • TBC: B60668

COUNTDOWN TO THE SECOND COMING:
A CHRONOLOGY OF PROPHETIC EARTH EVENTS
HAPPENING NOW —*Dave Hunt*

At last—a book that presents, in concise form, the events leading up to the return of Christ! In his characteristic direct style, Dave Hunt answers these pervasive questions: Who is the Antichrist? How will he be recognized? What current events indicate that we really are in the last days of the "last days"? For those who seek to understand the times from a biblical perspective, this summary of historic world events will excite, encourage, and equip God's people to boldly proclaim the Gospel to this generation. With clarity and conviction, Dave dispels popular distortions of the Last Days, and demonstrates how believers can minister effectively without fear or anxeiety, "redeeming the time, because the days are evil" (Ephesians 5:15-16). The Berean Call, 96 pages.

ISBN: 1-928660-19-3 • TBC: B00193

SEEKING & FINDING GOD:
IN SEARCH OF THE TRUE FAITH —*Dave Hunt*

It is simply astonishing how many *millions* of otherwise seemingly intelligent people are willing to risk their eternal destiny upon less evidence than they would require for buying a car or selecting a healthy food item—yet the belief of so many, particularly in the area of religion, has no rational or factual foundation. With well-researched arguments and compelling proof, this book demonstrates that the issue of where one will spend eternity is not a matter of preference (like joining the Elks instead of the Lions). In fact, there is overwhelming evidence that we are eternal beings who will spend eternity somewhere. But where will it be? And how can we know? There is no more important question to be faced—and answered. The Berean Call, 160 pages.

ISBN:1-928660-23-1 • TBC: B04425

About The Berean Call

The Berean Call (TBC) is a nonprofit, nondenominational ministry which exists to:

ALERT believers in Christ to unbiblical teachings and practices impacting the church

EXHORT believers to give greater heed to biblical discernment and truth regarding teachings and practices being currently promoted in the church

SUPPLY believers with teaching, information, and materials which will encourage the love of God's truth, and assist in the development of biblical discernment

MOBILIZE believers in Christ to action in obedience to the scriptural command to "earnestly contend for the faith" (Jude 3)

IMPACT the church of Jesus Christ with the necessity for trusting the Scriptures as the only rule for faith, practice, and a life pleasing to God

A free monthly newsletter, THE BEREAN CALL, may be received by sending a request to: PO Box 7019, Bend, OR 97708; or by calling

1-800-937-6638

To register for free email updates, to access our digital archives, and to order a variety of additional resource materials online, visit us at:

www.thebereancall.org

BEND • OREGON